The Puzzle Emporium

Presents

Amazing Brain Teasers

THIS IS A CARLTON BOOK

This edition published in 2013
by Carlton Books Limited
20 Mortimer Street
London W1T 3JW

ISBN 978-1-78097-315-9

10 9 8 7 6 5 4 3 2 1

Printed and bound in Great Britain by CPI Group (UK) Ltd, Croydon CR0 4YY

THE PUZZLE EMPORIUM

PRESENTS

AMAZING BRAIN TEASERS

CARLTON
BOOKS

Contents

Welcome to the Puzzle Emporium ...

If you're looking to expand your mind and blow the dust off your brain cells, you've come to the right place. Roll up, ladies and gentlemen. Roll up your selves and your sleeves, and get stuck in to the most thrilling collection of brain teasers, conundrums and enigmas ever to grace the pages of this (and possibly any other) book. The Puzzle Emporium is a carnival of wonders and delights all specially designed to cater to your every mental whim.

Puzzles and riddles are as old as humanity. In every culture we know, there is evidence for recreational mental challenges, from the smallest, most isolated Amazon tribes down through the mists of time to the ancient societies of Sumeria and Babylonia.

To puzzle, ladies and gentlemen, is to be human.

But it's not just fun and games. There's a serious side. Our curiosity, our need to find out how things work, is the driving force behind social evolution. Without our mental ambition, none of this would ever have happened.

It's just as important on a personal level, too. Research has proven beyond doubt that "Use it or lose it" is not just for physical muscles. If you want to keep your mind sharp, you need to give it some lifting to do. Luckily, that's fun at the same time.

So dig in. Enjoy our puzzles. And reconnect with what it means to be human.

PUZZLES

1 The Judgement

A man is tried for the crime of murder and found guilty. The judge says, "This is the strangest case I have ever seen. By all the evidence you are guilty beyond any reasonable doubt, yet the law requires that I set you free."

What is the reason for the judge's decision?

2 Islanders

On the island of Alopecia, the following facts are true:

1) No two islanders have exactly the same number of hairs.
2) No islander has exactly 450 hairs.
3) There are more islanders than there are hairs on the head of any one islander.

What is the largest possible number of islanders on Alopecia?

3 The Clock-Watcher

George did not have a wristwatch, but he did have an accurate clock. However, he sometimes forgot to wind it. Once when this happened George went to his sister's house, passed the evening with her, went back home, and set his clock. How could he do this without knowing beforehand the length of the trip?

4 Mending The Chain

Alice has four pieces of gold chain, each consisting of three links. She wants to have the pieces joined together to make a necklace, but she is afraid she can't afford it. The jeweller eyes the four pieces of chain on his workbench. "I charge a pound to break a link and a pound to melt it together again. To fit the pieces together, I'll have to break and re-join four links. That will be eight pounds'"

Alice knew she had less than £7. "I haven't enough money," she said sadly. "I was hoping to wear the necklace to a party tonight, but I suppose that's out of the question." Alice gathered the pieces of chain and prepared to leave the shop.

Just then the jeweller said, "Wait, I've thought of another way."

Sure enough, he had. How did he do it, and how much did he charge?

5 Fast Fly

An expensive Ferrari is travelling at 30 mph on a head-on collision course with an equally expensive Maserati, which is being driven at a leisurely 20 mph. When the two cars are exactly 50 miles apart, a very fast fly leaves the front bumper of the Ferrari and travels toward the Maserati at 100 mph. When it reaches the Maserati, it instantly reverses direction and flies back to the Ferrari and continues winging back and forth between the rapidly approaching cars. At the moment the two cars collide, what is the total distance the fly has covered?

6 How Fast?

The Baja Road Race is 1,000 miles long. At the halfway point Speedy Gonzales calculates that he has been driving at an average speed of 50 miles per hour. How fast should he drive the second half of the race if he wants to attain an overall average of 100 miles per hour?

7 The Prisoners' Test

A wicked king amuses himself by putting three prisoners to a test. He takes three hats from a box containing five hats – three red hats and two white hats. He puts one hat on each prisoner, leaving the remaining two hats in the box. He informs the men of the total number of hats of each colour, then says, "I want you men to try to determine the colour of the hat on your own head. The first man who does so correctly – and can explain his reasoning – will immediately be set free. But if any of you answers incorrectly, you will be executed on the spot."

The first man looks at the other two, and says, "I don't know."

The second man looks at the hats on the first and third man, and finally says, "I don't know the colour of my hat, either."

The third man is at something of a disadvantage. He is blind. But he is also clever. He thinks for a few seconds and then announces, correctly, the colour of his hat.

What colour hat is the blind man wearing? How did he know?

What Are They?

"How much will one cost?" asked the customer.
"Two pounds," replied the shopkeeper.
"And how much will twelve cost?"
"Four pounds."
"Okay. I'll take nine hundred and twelve."
"That will be six pounds please."

QUESTION: What was the customer buying?

What Comes Next?

What is the next letter in the following series?

O T T F F S S

Product

What is the product of the following series?

$$(x - a)(x - b)(x - c) \dots (x - z)$$

Speed Test

Complete this equation:

$$\frac{1234567890}{1234567891^2 - (1234567890 \times 1234567892)} = ?$$

Buttons And Boxes

Imagine you have three boxes, one containing two red buttons, one containing two green buttons, and the third, one red button and one green button. The boxes are labelled according to their contents – RR, GG and RG. However, the labels have been switched so that each box is now incorrectly labelled. Without looking inside, you may take one button at a time out of any box. Using this process of sampling, what is the smallest number of drawings needed to determine the contents of all three boxes?

13 Edgware and Euston

Sharon lives in Hampstead, near the tube station. She has two boyfriends, Wayne in Edgware and Kevin in Euston. To visit Wayne she takes a train from the northbound platform; to visit Kevin she takes a train from the southbound platform. Since Sharon likes both boys equally well, she simply gets on the first train that comes along. In this way she allows chance to determine whether she goes to Edgware or Euston. Sharon reaches the tube station at a random moment every Saturday afternoon. The northbound and southbound trains arrive at the station equally often – every 10 minutes. Yet for some reason she finds herself spending most of her time with Wayne in Edgware. In fact, on average she goes there nine times out of ten. Can you explain why the odds are so heavily in favour of Wayne?

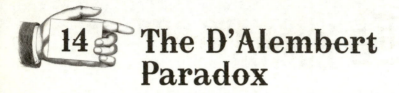

14 The D'Alembert Paradox

The French mathematician d'Alembert (1717-83) considered the probability of throwing heads at least once when tossing a coin twice. "There are only three possible cases," he argued: "(a) Tails appears on the first toss and again on the second toss, (b) Tails appears on the first toss and heads on the second toss, (c) Heads appears on the first toss (therefore in this case there is no longer need to carry out the second toss)."

"It is quite simple," he stated, "because there are only three possible cases and as two of these are favourable, the probability is 2/3." Was his reasoning correct?

15 Painted Faces

Wearied by their disputations and oppressed by the summer heat, three Greek philosophers lay down for a little nap under a tree in the Academy. As they slept a practical joker smeared their faces with black paint. Presently they all awoke at once and each began to laugh at the other. Suddenly one of them stopped laughing, for he realized that his own face was painted. What was his reasoning?

16 Cash Flow

A man spends $1/3$ of his money and loses $2/3$ of the remainder. He then has 12 pieces. How much money had he at first?

17 How Long?

A bolt of cloth is coloured as follows: $1/3$ and $1/4$ of it are black, and the remaining 8 yards are grey. How long is the bolt?

18 The Cloak

A servant is promised £100 and a cloak as his wages for a year. After 7 months he leaves this service, and receives the cloak and £20 as his due. How much is the cloak worth?

19 Two Steamers

Two steamers simultaneously leave New York for Lisbon, where they spend 5 days before returning to New York. The first makes 30 miles an hour going and 40 miles an hour returning. The second makes 35 miles an hour each way. Which steamer gets back first?

20 The Orchard

While three watchmen were guarding an orchard, a thief slipped in and stole some apples. On his way out he met the three watchmen one after the other, and to each in turn he gave a half of the apples he then had, and two besides. Thus he managed to escape with one apple. How many had he stolen originally?

21 Arithmetic Problem

In order to encourage his son in the study of arithmetic, a father agrees to pay his boy 8 pence for every problem correctly solved and to fine him 5 pence for each incorrect solution. At the end of 26 problems neither owes anything to the other. How many problems did the boy solve correctly?

22 Water Lentils

The water lentil reproduces by dividing into 2 every day. Thus on the first day we have 1, on the second 2, on the third 4, on the fourth 8, and so on. If, starting with one lentil, it takes 30 days to cover a certain area, how long will it take to cover the same area if we start with 2 lentils?

23 Wiring The House

Timothy has been abandoned by his electrician and must finish the wiring of his new house alone.

He courageously tries to untangle the labyrinth of wires already laid down. He is particularly worried about three wires of the same colour going from the basement to the attic. He wants to identify them, labelling both the basement and attic ends of one wire A, of another wire B, and of the last wire C.

His only tool is a meter that shows if current is passing through a length of wire or not when both ends of the wire are attached to the meter. Thanks to it, Timothy only needs to make one round trip between basement and attic to complete the labelling. Explain how he does it.

The Long Division

I was sitting before my chessboard pondering a combination of moves. At my side were my son, a boy of eight, and my daughter, four years old. The boy was busy with his homework, which consisted of some exercises in long division, but he was rather handicapped by his mischievous sister, who kept covering up his figures with chessmen. As I looked up, only two digits remained visible.

Can you calculate the missing digits without removing the chessmen?

25 The Truel

Lord Montcrief, Sir Henry Darlington and the Baron of Rockall decided to resolve a quarrel by fighting an unusual sort of pistol duel. They drew lots to determine who fired first, who second and who third. They then took their places at the corners of an equilateral triangle. It was agreed that they would fire single shots in turn and continue in the same order until two of them were dead. The man whose turn it was to fire could aim at either of the other two. It was known that Lord Montcrief always hit his target, that Sir Henry was 80 per cent accurate and the Baron was only 50 per cent accurate.

Assuming that all three adopted the best strategy, and that no one was killed by a wild shot not intended for him, which one had the best chance of surviving?

26 Missiles On Target

Two missiles, 1,250 miles apart, are fired directly at each other. One travels at 9,000 miles per hour and the other at 21,000 miles per hour. How far apart will they be exactly one minute before they collide?

27 Fair Shares

'Der Eine dielet, der Andere kieset.'

This is an old German saying which prescribes how to divide a cake between two people and ensure that both of them are satisfied. The translation is:

'One divides, the other chooses.'

Can you devise a procedure so that N persons can divide a cake between them and each one is satisfied that he has obtained at least 1/N of the cake?

28 Generosity

A generous man set aside a certain sum of money for equal distribution every week amongst those friends of his who were feeling the pinch. One day he remarked, "If there are five fewer applicants next week, you will each receive $20 more." Unfortunately, instead of there being fewer there were actually four more persons applying for the gift. "This means," he pointed out, "that you will each receive $10 less."

How much did each person receive at that last distribution?

29 The Striking Clock

It takes a clock two seconds to strike two o'clock, how long will it take to strike three o'clock?

30 The River

A man takes his motorboat to roar down a river to his pub. Going with the current he can cover the two kilometres in two minutes. Returning against the current, which is steady, it takes him four minutes. How long does it take him at slack water when there is no current?

31 Racing Driver

A racing driver drove around a 6-mile track at 140 mph for three miles, 168 mph for 1.5 miles, and 210 mph for 1.5 miles. What was his average speed for the entire 6 miles?

32 Changing The Odds

In a distant kingdom lived a king who had a beautiful daughter, who fell in love with a humble peasant boy whom she wanted to marry. The king had no intention of consenting, but suggested they leave the decision to chance. The three were standing in the castle's forecourt, which was covered with innumerable white and black pebbles. The king pretended to pick one of each colour, and put the two pebbles into his hat. The peasant boy was poor, but not stupid. He noticed that the king had picked two black pebbles. The suitor had to pick one pebble out of the hat. If it was white, he could marry the king's daughter. If black, he was never to see her again.

How could he extricate himself from this situation, without calling the king a cheat?

33 Two Cans

You have two cans filled with water and a large empty container. Is there a way to put all the water into the large container so that you can tell which water came from which can?

34 Zeno's Paradox

In the 5th century BC, Zeno, using his knowledge of infinity, sequences and partial sums, developed this famous paradox. He proposed that in a race with Achilles, a tortoise be given a head start of 1000 metres. Assume Achilles could run 10 times faster than the tortoise. When the race started and Achilles had gone 1000 metres, the tortoise would still be 100 metres ahead. When Achilles had gone the next 100 metres the tortoise would be 10 metres ahead.

Zeno argued that Achilles would continually gain on the tortoise, but he would never reach him. Was his reasoning correct? If Achilles were to pass the tortoise, at what point of the race would it be?

35 Handshakes

Is the number of people in the world who have shaken hands with an odd number of people odd or even?

36 The Boy And The Girl

A boy and a girl are talking.
'I'm a boy,' says the one with black hair.
'I'm a girl,' says the one with red hair.
If at least one of them is lying, which is which?

37 Hats In The Wind

Ten people, all wearing hats, were walking along a street when a sudden wind blew their hats off. A helpful boy retrieved them and, without asking which hat belonged to which person, handed each person a hat. What is the probability that exactly nine of the people received their own hats?

The Train And The Tunnel

A mile-long train is moving at sixty miles an hour when it reaches a mile-long tunnel. How long does it take the entire train to pass through?

39 The Waterlily

Waterlilies on a certain lake double in area every twenty-four hours. From the time the first waterlily appears until the lake is completely covered takes sixty days. On what day it is half-covered?

40 The Hill And The Bicycle

A bicycle climbs a certain hill at 10 miles an hour and returns at 20 miles an hour. What is its average speed for the entire trip?

 # 41 The Brick

A brick balances evenly with three quarters of a pound and three quarters of a brick. What does the whole brick weigh?

 # 42 A Unique Number

The following number is the only one of its kind. Can you figure out what is so special about it?

8,549,176,320

 # 43 Can You?

We eat what we can, and we can what we can't.'
Can you explain who could make this statement.

44 The Boss And His Chauffeur

A chauffeur always arrives at the train station at exactly five o'clock to pick up his boss and drive him home. One day his boss arrives an hour early, starts walking home, and is eventually picked up. He arrives at home twenty minutes earlier than usual. How long did he walk before he met his chauffeur?

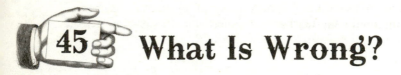

45 What Is Wrong?

Why are these statements obviously untrue?

1) There is a letter framed in Buckingham House signed "All my love, King William I"
2) Astronauts in their flights around the earth are always most tired when they see the sunset.
3) The first thing the Pilgrim Fathers did when they landed was to plant the Stars and Stripes near Plymouth Rock.
4) An archaeologist digging in Britain found a Roman coin dated 55 BC.

46 The Lock

"I believe you are unfamiliar with the penal system in our country," said the warden, as he led the new prisoner to his cell. "We find that it improves prison morale for each prisoner to have a chance to end his sentence at any time. In your case, we have set up a combination lock on your cell door. There are five dials, on which you can set up any five-digit number. If you can estimate within a margin of error of plus or minus twenty per cent the number of possible combinations you will be free to leave. You have ten minutes to respond."

The prisoner knew nothing about permutations, but being intelligent, worked out the answer within seconds.

47 The Weather Report

"Can you tell me what the temperature has been at noon for the past five days?" John asked the weatherman.

"I don't exactly recall," replied the weatherman, "but I do remember that the temperature was different each day, and that the product of the temperatures is 12."

Assuming that the temperatures are expressed to the nearest degree, what were the five temperatures?

48 Two Sizes Of Apple

A man had an apple stall and he sold his larger apples at 3 for a dollar and his smaller apples at 5 for a dollar. When he had just 30 apples of each size left to sell, he asked his son to look after the stall while he had lunch. When he came back from lunch the apples were all gone and the son gave his father $15. The father questioned his son. "You should have received $10 for the large apples and $6 for the 30 small apples, making $16 in all." The son looked surprised. "I am sure I gave you all the money I received and I counted the change most carefully. It was difficult to manage without you here, and, as there was an equal number of each sized apple left, I sold them all at the average price of 4 for $1. Four into 60 goes 15 times so I am sure $15 is correct."

Where did the $1 go?

49 Presidents

"Here is an odd item, Professor Flugel," said Tom, looking up from his newspaper. "It says here that three of the first five presidents of the United States died on the Fourth of July. I wonder what the odds are against a coincidence like that."

"I'm not sure," replied the professor, "but I'm willing to give ten-to-one odds I can name one of the three who died on that date."

Assuming that the professor had no prior knowledge of the dates on which any of the presidents died, was he justified in offering such odds?

50 Jim And George

How is it possible for Jim to stand behind George and George to stand behind Jim at the same time?

51 A Chiming Clock

A clock chimes every hour on the hour, and once each quarter hour in between. If you hear it chime once, what is the longest you may have to wait to be sure what time it is?

52 The Half-Full Barrel

Two farmers were staring into a large barrel partly filled with ale. One of them said: "It's over half full!" But the other declared: "It's more than half empty." How could they tell without using a ruler, string, bottles, or other measuring devices if it was more or less than exactly half full?

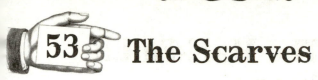

53 The Scarves

The King's daughters were skilled in weaving, and their scarves were a matter of near-legendary debate.

Eleanor, Marian and Guinevere prided themselves on their talents, and were fiercely competitive as to whose work was superior. It was not just a matter of warmth, or lightness of the garment, or even how swiftly a scarf could be made, but rather a tangled question of all three.

Eleanor could make five scarves in the same time that Marian made two, but while Eleanor was making three scarves, Guinevere would have made four.

Just one of Eleanor's scarves weighed as much as five of Guinevere's, but three of Guinevere's weighed as much as five of Marian's.

Four of Guinevere's scarves were required to get the same warmth as one of Marian's, but just one of Eleanor's was as warm as three of Marian's.

Obviously, different people prized different things in a scarf. But if you were to give equal importance to rapidity, lightness and warmth, which sister would you judge to be the finest weaver?

54 The Marksman

One marksman can fire 5 shots in 5 seconds while another can get off 10 shots in 10 seconds. (We will assume that timing starts when the first shot is fired and ends with the last shot, but the shots themselves will be assumed to take no time.)

Which man can fire 12 shots in a shorter time?

55 The Marbles

Two bags each contain 3 red, 3 white, and 3 blue marbles. Without looking, someone removes from the first bag the largest number of marbles that it is possible to remove while still being sure that at least one of each colour remains. These marbles are put into the second bag. Now he transfers back (without looking, of course) the smallest possible number of marbles that will assure there being at least 2 of each colour in the first bag.

How many marbles remain in the second bag?

The Square Table

A square table is constructed with an obstruction in the middle of it, so that when 4 people are seated one of each side, each can see his neighbours to right and left but not the person seated directly across. The 4 people seated at this table were told to raise their hands if, when looking to the right and left, they saw at least one woman. They were also told to announce the sex of the one person whom they could not see, if it could be figured out logically.

Since, as a matter of fact, all 4 people were women, each raised her hand, but then several minutes went by before one of them announced that she was certain that the person seated opposite her was a woman.

How could she logically have come to that conclusion?

A Carbon Copy

For some reason, probably dishonest, someone wants to write a letter that will appear to be a carbon copy. He has only one sheet of paper and one piece of carbon paper, which he places under the letter paper with the carbon side facing the back of the sheet.

He then writes with a pen which has no ink so the writing will appear only on the underside of the paper. Note that normal writing would make the writing appear abnormal, so he decides to write abnormally. Instead of the usual F, for example, he writes Ⅎ; instead of R, he writes Я, etc.

Should he start the letter in the upper left-hand corner, upper right, lower right, or lower left?

58 Walking In Step

A man and woman, out walking together, both start out by taking a step with the left foot. In order to keep together, the man, whose stride is longer, takes 2 steps while the woman takes 3.

How many steps will the woman have taken when they are both about to step out together with their right feet for the first time?

59 The Hunter

A hunter was hunting alone and he was running short of food. Luckily he met two shepherds, one of whom had three small loaves and the other five. When the hunter asked them for food, they agreed to divide the loaves equally among the three of them. The hunter thanked them for the food and paid the shepherds 8 piasters.

How did the shepherds divide the money?

60 Unusual Equations

a) 5 + 5 + 5 = 550
   Using a line equal to a hyphen, ie '-' in any position,
   rectify the above equation.
b) Using four nines, make them equal 100.
c) Do the same with four sevens.
d) Arrange three nines to equal 20.

61 Family Matters

A man and his wife had three children, John, Ben, and
Mary, and the difference between their parents' ages was
the same as between John and Ben and between Ben and
Mary.

The ages of John and Ben, multiplied together, equalled
the age of the father, and the ages of Ben and Mary
multiplied together equalled the age of the mother. The
combined ages of the family amounted to ninety years.

What was the age of each person?

62 The Gambler

Someone has a sum of money, one-third of which he spends. Two-thirds of the remainder he loses at dice, leaving 12 dollars in his pocket. How much money did he have originally?

63 Fly Around the World

There are a number of planes on an island. The fuel tank of each plane, when filled, contains enough fuel to take it halfway around the world. It is possible to transfer fuel from one plane to another during flight, but there is no other source of fuel available. The pilots are told that one plane must fly around the world and that every plane must return to the island.

Now, we can see that no one plane can fly around by itself; it needs help from others, which can transfer fuel to it during the flight.

What is the absolute minimum number of planes needed so that one of them can fly around the world?

64 The Collector's Bequest

A rich collector of gold coins left a very complicated will giving instructions as to how his gold coin collection (less than 5,000) was to be distributed to his ten children, five sons and five daughters, after his death. The instructions he gave were that first of all one gold coin was to be given to his butler, then exactly a fifth of those remaining had to go to his eldest son. Another coin was then given to the butler, then exactly a fifth of those still remaining went to his second eldest son. This procedure was then repeated exactly until all his five sons had received a share, and the butler had been given five gold coins. Then, after the fifth son had taken his share the gold coins still remaining were to be equally divided between his five daughters.

How many gold coins did the collector have in his collection?

65 Jugs

There are many variations of puzzles involving decanting (pouring from one container to another). The one we present here is known to be at least 400 years old.

The three jugs have capacity for 8, 5 and 3 pints respectively. The 8-pint jug is filled entirely with water and the other two jugs are empty. Your task is, by decanting, to divide the water into two equal parts, ie 4 pints in jug A and 4 pints in jug B, leaving the smallest jug empty. None of the jugs is calibrated so the only way the task can be successfully performed is to pour water from one jug to another until the first jug is entirely empty or the second jug is entirely full. You must assume that the decanting is done with great care so that no water is spilled.

What is the least number of decantings in which the task can be achieved?

66 A Bottle Of Wine

A bottle of wine costs £10. If the wine is worth £9 more than the bottle, what is the value of the bottle.

67 One-Two-Three

We first heard of this puzzle from a Mensa member who had come across it years before at a mathematical conference in Holland. We gave the puzzle to a friend of ours who could not solve it and took it along to his club. The members there pondered over it for many hours without success. Finally one member took it home to show his twelve-year-old son, who solved it in five minutes. It is that type of puzzle.

What is the next row of digits below?

1									
1	1								
2	1								
1	2	1	1						
1	1	1	2	2	1				
3	1	2	2	1	1				
1	3	1	1	2	2	2	1		
1	1	1	3	2	1	3	2	1	1
?	?	?	?	?	?	?	?	?	?

68 Men In A Circle

This puzzle was one of a series which Lewis Carroll called his pillow-problems, which were almost all compiled while lying awake at night. He would commit nothing to paper until the morning, when he would first of all write down the answer, followed by the question and then the detailed solution.

Some men sat in a circle, so that each had two neighbours; and each had a certain number of shillings. The first had 1 shillings more than the second, who had 1 shilling more than the third, and so on. The first gave 1 shilling to the second, who gave 2 shillings to the third, and so on, each giving 1 shilling more than he received, as long as possible. There were then two neighbours, one of whom had four times as much as the other. How many men were there? And how much had the poorest man at first?

69 Handicap Race

Two men run a race of 100 yards which Man A wins by 5 yards. Because of this they decide to have a re-run and this time instigate a handicapping system whereby Man A starts the race 5 yards behind the starting line, thereby giving Man B a 5 yard start. Both men run the second race at exactly the same speed as before. What was the result?

Gold Card

This puzzle was a favourite of the Wild West card-sharps and thousands of dollars were won from unsuspecting gold prospectors. In a saloon the gambler would gather a crowd and into a hat would place three cards. These cards were coloured:

GOLD on one side	**GOLD on reverse**
SILVER on one side	**SILVER on reverse**
GOLD on one side	**SILVER on reverse**

The gambler then asked an onlooker to draw a card from the hat and place it on the table, and then he would pull out the silver/silver card himself, and show it around.

Then the gambler said: "The reverse side is either gold or silver as the card cannot be the silver/silver card. Therefore it is either the gold/silver card or the gold/gold card, an even chance! I will bet even money one dollar that the reverse side is gold." (If the silver/silver card was not available, the exact process could be duplicated with the gold/gold card.)

Is this a fair bet?

71 The Missing £

This is a very old English puzzle. Three men dined in a restaurant and the bill came to £25.

Each man gave the waiter £10 and told him to keep £2 out of the change as a tip.

The waiter returned with £3 and proceeded to give each man £1.

The meal had therefore cost £27 plus £2 for the waiter's tip. Where had the other £1 gone?

72 A Digital Puzzle

What arithmetic symbol can we place between 2 and 3 to make a number greater than 2 but less than 3?

The Aeroplane

An aeroplane flies in a straight line from airport A to airport B, then back in a straight line from B to A. It travels with a constant engine speed and there is no wind. Will its travel time for the same round trip be greater, less or the same if, throughout both flights, at the same engine speed, a constant wind blows from A to B?

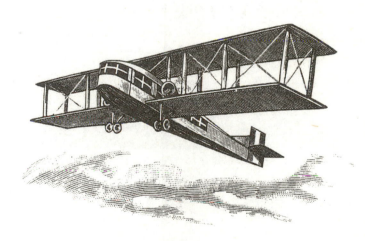

74 Drive-By

"I was walking along the road at three and a half miles an hour," said Mr. Desborough, "when the car dashed past me and only missed me by a few inches. I could have sworn the chap inside was carrying a pistol!"

"Do you know at what speed it was going?" asked his friend.

"Well, from the moment it passed me to its disappearance round a corner took twenty-seven steps and walking on reached that corner with one hundred and thirty-five steps more."

"Then, assuming that you walked, and the car ran, each at a uniform rate, we can easily work out the speed."

Walking Home

John was going home from Brighton. He rode half way –
fifteen times as fast as he goes on foot. The second half he
went by ox team. He can walk twice as fast as that.
Would he have saved time if he had gone all the way
on foot? If so, how much?

Four Insects

Four insects – A, B, C and D – occupy the corners of a
square 10 inches on a side. A and C are male, B and D
are female. Simultaneously A crawls directly towards B,
B towards C, C towards D and D towards A. If all insects
crawl at the same constant rate, they will describe four
congruent logarithmic spirals which meet at the centre of
the square.

How far does each insect travel before they meet?
The problem can be solved without calculus.

Changing Money

Here is that very puzzling story having to do with foreign exchange. The governments of two neighbouring countries – let's call them Eastland and Westland – had an agreement whereby an Eastland dollar was worth a dollar in Westland, and vice versa. But one day the government of Eastland decreed that thereafter a Westland dollar was to be worth but ninety cents in Eastland. The next day the Westland government, not to be outdone, decreed that thereafter an Eastland dollar was to be worth but ninety cents in Westland.

Now a young entrepreneur named Malcolm lived in a town which straddled the border between the two countries. He went into a store on the Eastland side, bought a ten-cent razor, and paid for it with an Eastland dollar. He was given a Westland dollar, worth ninety cents there, in change. He then crossed the street, went into a Westland store, bought a ten-cent package of blades, and paid for it with the Westland dollar. There he was given an Eastland dollar in change. When Malcolm returned home, he had his original dollar and his purchases. And each of the tradesmen had ten cents in his cash-drawer.

Who, then, paid for the razor and blades?

78 A Pair Of Socks

28 black socks and 28 brown socks are inside a drawer in a dark room. What is the minimum number of socks that I must take out of the drawer to guarantee that I have a matching pair?

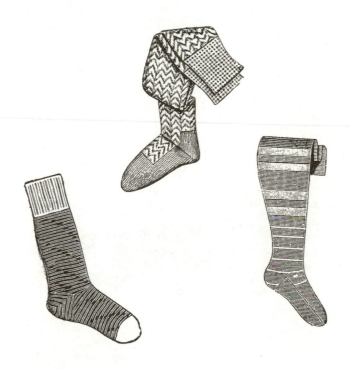

79 The Slow Horses

An aged and, it appears, somewhat eccentric king wants to pass his throne on to one of his two sons. He decrees that a horse race shall be held and that the son who owns the slower horse shall become king. The sons, each fearing that the other will cheat by having his horse go less fast than it is capable of, ask a wise man's advice. With only two words the wise man ensures that the race will be fair.

What does he say?

80 Hourglass

You have two hourglasses – a four-minute glass and a seven-minute glass. You want to measure nine minutes. How do you do it?

81 Double The Bottle

A quart bottle had all its dimensions doubled. What is the volume of the new bottle?

82 Sorting Numbers

Which groups do these three numbers belong in:

15, 16, 17 ?

Group 1: 36, 88, 90
Group 2: 11, 14, 71
Group 3: 25, 76, 92

83 Categories

The letters of the alphabet can be grouped into four distinct classes. The first thirteen letters establish the categories:

A M
B C D E K
F G J L
H I

Place the remaining thirteen letters in their proper categories.

84 Rope Trick

Two flagpoles are each 100 feet high. A rope 150 feet long is strung between the tops of the flagpoles. At its lowest point the rope sags to within 25 feet of the ground. How far apart are the flagpoles?

What Weights?

A boy selling fruit has only three weights, but with them he can weigh any whole number of pounds from 1 pound to 13 pounds inclusive. What weights has he?

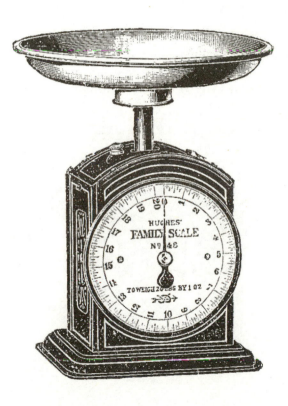

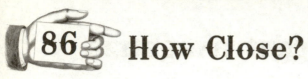

86 How Close?

What is the closest relation that your mother's brother's brother-in-law could be to you?

87 Decafiné

This is to be solved in the head, without paper and pencil. If some coffee is '97% caffeine-free,' how many cups of it would one have to drink to get the amount of caffeine in a cup of regular coffee?

88 Eggstravaganza

If a hen and a half lays an egg and a half in a day and a half, then how many and a half who lay better by half will lay half a score and a half in a week and a half?

89 How Many Hops

You are standing at the centre of a circle of radius 9 feet. You begin to hop in a straight line to the circumference. Your first hop is 4 $\frac{1}{2}$ feet, your second 2 $\frac{1}{4}$ feet, and you continue to hop each time half the length of your previous hop. How many hops will you make before you get out of the circle?

90 The Painting

A man, looking at a painting, says to himself: "Brothers and sisters have I none, but that man's father is my father's son."

Who is the man in the painting?

91 The Watchmaker

A watchmaker was telephoned urgently to make a house call to replace the broken hands of a clock. He was sick, so he sent his apprentice.

The apprentice was thorough. When he finished inspecting the clock it was dark. He hurriedly attached the new hands, but mixed up the hour and the minute hands. He then set the clock by his pocket watch. It was six o'clock, so he set the big hand at 12 and the little hand at 6.

The apprentice returned, but soon the telephone rang. He picked up the receiver only to hear the client's angry voice:

"You didn't do the job right. The clock shows the wrong time."

Surprised, he hurried back to the client's house. He found the clock showing not much past eight. He handed his watch to the client, saying: "Check the time, please. Your clock is not off even by 1 second."

The client had to agree.

Early next morning the client telephoned to say that the clock hands, having apparently gone berserk, were moving around the clock at will. When the apprentice rushed over, the clock showed a little past seven. After checking with his watch, the apprentice got angry:

"You are making fun of me! You clock shows the right time!"

Do you know what was going on?

92 Birthdates

If there were twenty-four people in a room and you bet that at least one coincidence of birth dates existed would you have a better chance of winning or losing your bet?

93 The Lead Plate

The builders of an irrigation canal needed a lead plate of a certain size, but had no lead in stock. They decided to melt some lead shot. But how could they find its volume beforehand?

One suggestion was to measure a ball, apply the formula for the volume of a sphere, and multiply by the number of balls. But this would take too long, and anyway the shot wasn't all the same size.

Another was to weigh all the shot and divide by the specific gravity of lead. Unfortunately, no one could remember this ratio, and there was no manual in the field shop.

Another was to pour the shot into a gallon jar. But the volume of the jug is greater than the volume of the shot by an undetermined amount, since the shot cannot be packed solid and part of the jug contains air.

Do you have a suggestion?

94 The Callipers

A student had to measure a cylindrical machine part with indentations at its bases.

He had no depth gauge, only callipers and a ruler. The problem was, he could find the distance between the indentations with the callipers, but he would have to remove the callipers to measure their spread on the ruler. But to remove the callipers he would have to open the legs, and then there would be nothing to measure.

What did he do?

95 The Wire's Diameter

At technical school we study the construction of lathes and machines. We learn how to use instruments and how not to be stumped by difficult situations.

My foreman-teacher handed me some wire and asked: 'How do you measure the wire's diameter?'
'With a micrometer gauge.'
'And if you don't have one?'
On thinking it over, I had an answer. What was it?

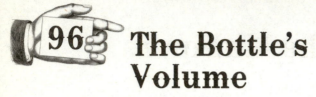

96 The Bottle's Volume

If a bottle, partly filled with liquid, has a round, square or rectangular bottom which is flat, can you find its volume using only a ruler? You may not add or pour out liquid.

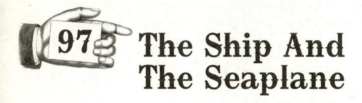

97 The Ship And The Seaplane

A diesel ship leaves on a long voyage. When it is 180 miles from shore, a seaplane, whose speed is ten times that of the ship, is sent to deliver mail.

How far from shore does the seaplane catch up with the ship?

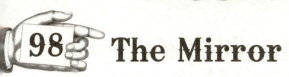

98 The Mirror

We all know that a mirror reverses you (apparently) from left-to-right, but not head-to-foot. But do you know why?

99 The Ships And The Lifebuoy

Two diesel ships leave a pier simultaneously, the Neptune downstream and the Poseidon upstream, with the same motive force.

As they leave, a lifebuoy falls off the Neptune and floats downstream. An hour later both ships are ordered to reverse course.

Will the Neptune's crew be able to pick up the buoy before the ships meet?

100 Equations To Solve In Your Head

Solve this pair of simultaneous equations to find x and y.

$$6,751x + 3,249y = 26,751$$
$$3,249x + 6,751y = 23,249$$

Three Men in The Street

Three men met on the street – Mr Black, Mr Grey and Mr White.

"Do you know," asked Mr Black, "that between us we are wearing black, grey and white? Yet not one of us is wearing the colour of his name?"

"Why, that's right," said the man in white.

Can you say who was wearing which colour?

Sisters

Two look-alike girls sitting on a bench in the park are approached by a stranger.

"You must be twins", says he. The girls smile. "We have the same parents and were born on the same day in the same year, and yet we are not twins."

Explain.

103 The Telephone Call

"Hello. Is this XYZ 9876?"

"Yes. Who is calling, please?"

"What? You don't recognize my voice, young woman? Why, my mother is your mother's mother-in-law."

"Huh?"

What is the relationship of the speakers?

104 Relations

"Jean is my niece," said Jack to his sister Jill. "She is not my niece," said Jill.
  Can you explain?

105 Aborigines

Two Australian Aborigines were sitting on a rock – a big Aborigine and a little Aborigine. The little Aborigine was the son of the big Aborigine, but the big Aborigine was not the father of the little Aborigine.

Explain!

106 Sons' Ages?

Two people were talking. One said to the other, "I have three sons whose ages I want you to ascertain from the following clues:

The sum of their ages is 13.

The product of their ages is the same as your age.

My oldest son weighs 61 pounds."

The Dinner Party

In the narrative Eligible Apartments, Lewis Carroll posed the following puzzle:

The Governor of Kgovjni wants to give a very small dinner-party, and invites his father's brother-in-law, his brother's father-in-law, his father-in-law's brother, and his brother-in-law's father.

Find the smallest possible number of guests.

108 Four Families

"Are those your children playing in the garden?" asked the visitor.

"There are in fact four families of children," replied the host. "Mine is the largest, my brother's family is smaller, my sister's is smaller still, and my cousin's is the smallest of all. He went on, "They wanted to play baseball but there are not enough children to make two teams. Curiously enough, the product of the numbers in the four groups is my house number, which you saw when you came in."

"Let me see," said the visitor, "whether I can find the number of children in the various families." After thinking for a time he said, "I need more information. Does your cousin's family consist of a single child?" The host answered his question, whereupon the visitor said, "Knowing your house number and knowing the answer to my question, I can now deduce the exact number of children in each family."

How many children were there in each of the four families, and what was the reply to the visitor's question?

109 Father And Grandfather

Is it possible for one's grandfather to be younger than one's father?

110 Husbands And Fathers

Mary and Joan met in the supermarket and started to chat:

"The other night, a curious thought occurred to me," said Mary to Joan. "Do you realize that we have a strange relationship? Our fathers are our husbands, and they are also the fathers of our children."

Explain.

How Many Children?

Each son in the Hubbard family has just as many brothers as sisters, but each daughter has twice as many brothers as sisters. How many boys and how many girls are there in the family?

112 Boys And Girls

A sultan wanted to increase the proportion of women to men in the population of his country so that the men could have larger harems. He proposed to accomplish this by passing a law which forbade a woman from having any more children as soon as she had given birth to a male child. Thus, he reasoned, some families would have several girls and only one boy, but no family could have more than one boy. After a time, females would outnumber males. Or would they?

113 Two Children

I have two children. At least one of them is a boy. What is the probability that both my children are boys?

My sister also has two children. The older child is a girl. What is the probability that both her children are girls?

The Surgeon

A well-dressed man, let's call him John, in his forties, enters a bar in Manhattan.

After looking around, he sits down next to a shabbily-dressed man who is obviously the worse for drink. John strikes up a conversation and orders more drinks. After some small talk, John makes the following proposition to the stranger: "I am Dr John Hopkins, and I am a qualified surgeon. If you let me amputate your left forearm, I will pay you $1,000,000 and will provide you with an artificial limb." After some hesitation, the stranger agrees and they proceed to John's surgery.

After the amputation John packs the limb in dry ice and sends the parcel to an address in Los Angeles. At the same time, he sends cables to a number of addresses on the West Coast. Several days later eight men meet in LA. The parcel is being opened, the men look at it, express satisfaction and disperse.

Find an explanation which will logically meet the circumstances.

115 Marital Problem

Jason and Dean were brothers. Jason married Jackie, and Dean married Denise.

However, Jason and Denise have the same wedding anniversary. Dean's wedding anniversary was one month before this date, and Jackie's was one month after it. There have been no divorces or remarriages. How do you explain this?

116 The Widow's Sister

There is this story about a man who had once married his widow's sister. Is this possible?

117 The Lift Stopped

A man leaves his apartment, situated on the tenth floor of a high-rise building.

He calls the lift and descends. Suddenly the lift stops between the fourth and third floors, and the light goes out. At that moment the man's face turns ashen and he exclaims: "Oh God, my wife is dying."

Explain.

118 The Car Crash

Mr Jim Jones was driving home in his car, with his son Robert in the passenger seat. The car was involved in a crash with a lorry, and Jim, the father, was killed outright. His son Robert was seriously injured and taken off to hospital in an ambulance. In the hospital operating theatre, the surgeon looked at Robert and said, "I'm sorry, but I can't operate on this patient – he is my son Robert."

What is the explanation?

The Barber's Shop

One day, late afternoon, a man, let's call him John, opens the door to a barber's shop in which only one man, the owner, serves his customers.

A man is being shaved, but there are three men waiting.

"How long will you be?" asks John. The barber, after a little reflection, replies,

"Oh, about an hour."

"Thank you" says John and leaves.

About the same time a few days later the same scenario occurs except that John's waiting time would have been reduced to 40 minutes. Again John acknowledges and leaves.

The following day, the barber is about to finish with a customer, and there is no one waiting. "I can take you straight away" says the barber. John is taken aback, but thanks and leaves the shop.

Explain.

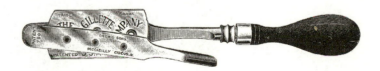

The Unfaithful Wife

John, the author, had suspected for some time that his wife Eva was unfaithful, though he had no proof.

One morning, as John was working on his latest novel, Eva mentioned that she intended to go to the cinema and would be out for a few hours. As Eva went to the door, John looked at her pensively, and then returned to his work.

Three hours later, Eva returned, took her coat off and asked John whether he wanted some coffee. When she returned from the kitchen, John asked her to sit down as he wanted to talk to her.

"Eva," he said, "I want a divorce."

Why?

121 The Bridge

A-town and B-town are two villages connected by a bridge spanning a river. At the end of a war, the occupying forces installed a sentry in the middle of the bridge to prevent the inhabitants of A-town and B-town from visiting each other.

All means of transport having been requisitioned, the only access to the other village was by foot over the bridge, which would take 10 minutes. The sentry was under strict orders to come out of his bunker every 5 minutes, and send anyone trying to cross back to his own village, if necessary by force of arms.

Michael in A-town was desperate to visit his girlfriend in B-town. How did he succeed?

122 A Safe Place

A man named George leaves home, and when he tries to return, a man wearing a mask blocks his path. George immediately turns around and runs to a safe place.

a) What is George doing?

b) What is the masked man's occupation?

c) Where is George's "safe place"?

123 The Last Movie

Tom and Joe go to a movie. During the picture they exchange angry words.

Tom draws a gun, Joe screams, and Tom shoots Joe dead. Tom gets out of his seat and leaves the theatre. The shooting and screaming did not coincide with loud noises in the movie soundtrack. Although there were many other people in the theatre, no one tried to stop Tom. Why didn't they?

124 The Last Letter

A woman is seated and writing a letter. There is a thunderstorm outside and she dies. How did she die?

125 Death In The Car

A man was shot to death while in his car. There were no powder marks on his clothing, which indicated that the gunman was outside the car. However, all the windows were closed up and the doors locked. After a closer inspection was made, the only bullet holes discovered were on the man's body. How was he murdered?

126 The Stranger

A married couple was speeding into town when their sedan ran out of gas. The man went for help after making sure his wife closed the windows and locked the doors of the car. Upon his return, he found his wife dead and a stranger in the car. The windows were still closed, the doors were still locked, and no damage was done to the car. How did the woman die, and who is the stranger?

127 The Heir

The king dies and two men, the true heir and an imposter, both claim to be his long-lost son. Both fit the description of the rightful heir: about the right age, height, colouring and general appearance. Finally, one of the elders proposes a test to identify the true heir. One man agreed to the test while the other flatly refused. The one who agreed was immediately sent on his way, and the one who refused was correctly identified as the rightful heir. Why?

The Antique Candelabra

The scene is a famous antique shop in London's Bond Street. A white Rolls Royce pulls up and a liveried chauffeur opens the door to an elegant, distinguished-looking elderly man, who enters the antique dealers.

He points at a 17th century candelabra in the window. He examines it closely and then engages in an animated dialogue with the owner of the shop. Eventually he writes a cheque for £5,000 and departs with the candelabra.

Shortly thereafter the owner makes a number of telephone calls before closing the shop. Two days later he receives a call, which clearly gets him excited.

In the mean time, the distinguished-looking man can be seen in his room at the Ritz, carefully wrapping the candelabra he had bought two days before. He hands it to a younger man, whom he calls Robert. Robert leaves the hotel, hails a taxi and goes to the same antique shop. There he hands the candelabra to the owner, who pays him £9,000 in cash. Can you explain?

A Soldier's Dream

A soldier had a dream that his king would be assassinated on his first visit to a foreign city. He pleaded with the king to cancel his visit, thinking the vision might be a horrible omen. The king pondered the man's advice for a moment and then ordered him taken away and beheaded. Why?

130 The Jilted Bride

In a mountain village in Switzerland one winter a couple were being married.

During the wedding a girl, jilted by the bridegroom, appeared and made a scene.

"The wedding bell will not ring," she said and immediately took poison and was rushed to hospital.

Sure enough when the bell-ringer tried, there was no sound from the bell. Some said she was a witch and had cast a spell but others thought she had tied the clapper. After the ceremony they went to the belfry but found everything in working order. There were no signs of anything that would prevent the bell from ringing. How had she stopped the bell ringing but left no trace?

131 The Careful Driver

I'm driving down a highway at the legal 55 mph limit. I'm sober; my licence plates, licence and insurance are in order; and I'm wearing my seat belt.

I passed three cars without going over 55 mph, but a state patrolman pulled me over and gave me a ticket. Why?

The Two Solicitors

Smith and Jones are partners in a small firm of solicitors dealing mostly with corporate clients. Jones had worked for a much larger organization but, as he became impatient with the slow pace of promotion, he had made a change.

Smith is eight years his junior and is working in the same office as Jones, acting effectively as his assistant.

One morning, just before noon, Jones' secretary burst into the office, full of excitement: "Mr Jones, the hospital just phoned, your wife has given birth to twins."

On hearing this, Smith paled, got hold of a paperweight and threw it at Jones.

Explain!

A Glass of Water

A man enters a bar and asks for a glass of water.
The bartender draws a gun and shoots into the ceiling.
The man thanks him and walks out.
Why?

134 The Deadly Scotch

Mr El and Mr Lay went into a bar and each ordered a scotch on the rocks.

Unbeknown to them, they both got glasses containing poison. Mr El downed his quickly and proceeded to gab for an hour while Mr Lay drank his slowly.

Later, Mr Lay died, but Mr El didn't. Why?

135 Bus Timetable

A man drives along a main road on which a regular service of buses is in operation. He notices that every three minutes he meets a bus and that every six minutes a bus overtakes him. How often does a bus leave the terminal station at one end of the route?

136 Above Or Below

The first twenty-five letters of the alphabet are written out, as shown - with some letters above the line and some below. Where should the Z go: above the line or below, and why?

A		EF	HI	KLMN		T	VWXY
	BCD		G	J		OPQRSU	

137 The Steelworker

David Miller, 45 years old, lives in a high-rise apartment building, within walking distance of the local steelworks where he is employed as plant supervisor.

Every morning at 8.00 a.m., he walks down a flight of stairs, and when he arrives at his destination he first makes himself a cup of tea. He then reads the morning paper, which he has picked up from the news-vendor at the corner. Half way through the paper, his eyelids get heavy and he falls asleep for a solid eight hours. Nonetheless, at the end of the month he is looking forward to a nice productivity-linked bonus.

How does he get away with it?

138 Rice Paper

Suppose we have a large sheet of very thin rice paper one-thousandth of an inch thick, or a thousand sheets to the inch. We tear the paper in half and put the two pieces together, one of top of the other. We tear them in half and put the four pieces together in a pile, tear them in half and put the eight pieces in a pile, and so on. If we tear and put together fifty times, how high will the final stack of paper be? The usual responses are amusing. Some people suggest a foot, others go as high as several feet, and a few bolder ones a mile. What do you think?

The Phone-In

Tom Bradley had left his home in Alperton early that day to drive to Manchester for a seminar, spread over three days.

Driving up the M1, he switched on the radio and listened to a phone-in programme whereby the moderator was telephoning London subscribers at random to obtain their views on the performance of public transport in the Greater London area.

Tom listened to three opinions with slight amusement, nodding his head in a gesture of approval when he agreed with a response.

Suddenly his face turned angry. He headed towards the next exit, and sped for home.

Explain.

SOLUTIONS

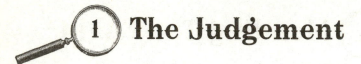

1 The Judgement

The man was one of Siamese twins.

2 Islanders

The answer is 450. Suppose there were more than 450 inhabitants – say 452. Then there would have to be 452 distinct numbers all less than 452 and none of them equal to 450 – which is impossible. There are exactly 452 distinct numbers (including zero) less than 452; hence there are only 451 numbers other than 450 that are less than 452.

Obviously one of the inhabitants of Alopecia must be bald.

3 The Clock-Watcher

When George left his house he started the clock and wrote down the time it then showed. When he got to his sister's house he noted the time when he arrived and the time when he left. He thus knew how long he was at his sister's house. When he got back home, he looked at the clock, so he knew how long he had been away from home. Subtracting from this the time he had spent at his sister's house, he knew how long the walk back and forth had been. By adding half of this to the time he left his sister's house, he then knew what time it really was now.

4) Mending The Chain

The jeweller cut all three links on one of the pieces, then he used the broken links to join the other segments. He charged £6.

5) Fast Fly

At first glance it may seem that a horrendous calculation is necessary to solve this: the sum of an infinite series of numbers that get smaller and smaller as the cars approach each other. But if you focus on time rather than distance, a solution is easy. The cars are 50 miles apart and travelling toward each other at a combined speed of 50 miles per hour, so they will meet in one hour. In that hour, a fly that goes 100 miles per hour will naturally travel 100 miles.

6) How Fast

Speedy will have to drive at an infinite speed in order to average 100 mph for the course. He must drive the whole 1,000 miles in ten hours to attain the required speed, but he has already used up his ten hours to drive the first half of the course. He will have to finish the race in zero time.

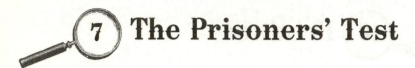

7 The Prisoners' Test

The blind man is wearing a red hat. His reasoning is as follows: "The first man did not see two white hats. If he had he would have known immediately that he was wearing a red hat because there are only two white hats. The second man, aware that the first did not see two white hats, needed only to look at me: If he saw a white hat on me, he would, therefore, know he wore a red hat. Since he didn't know, he must not have seen a white hat on me. Therefore, my hat must be red."

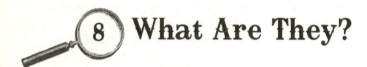

8 What Are They?

House numbers.

9 What Comes Next?

The letters are the initials of the first seven numbers: One, Two, Three, etc. The eighth letter, then, is E.

O T T F F S S E

10 Product

Since one of the terms in this series will be (x - x), which equals zero, the product of the entire series is zero.

11 Speed Test

Let 1234567891 be 'n'. Then the denominator can be written as:

$$n^2 - [(n - 1) \times (n + 1)], \text{ or } n^2 - n^2 + 1 = 1$$

Therefore the answer is 1234567890.

12 Buttons and Boxes

You can ascertain the contents of all three boxes by taking out just one button. The solution depends on the fact that the labels on all three boxes are incorrect. Take a button from the box labelled RG. Assume that the button removed is red. You now know that the other button in this box must be red also, otherwise the label would be correct. Since you have identified which box contains two red buttons, you can work out immediately the contents of the box marked GG because you know it cannot contain two green buttons since its label has to be wrong. It cannot contain two red buttons, for you have already identified that box. Therefore it must contain one red and one green button. The third box, of course, must then be the one with the two green buttons. The same reasoning works if the first button you take from the RG box happens to be green instead of red.

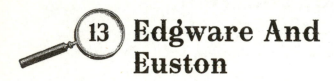

13 Edgware And Euston

While the Edgware and Euston trains arrive equally often – every 10 minutes – it so happens that the Euston train always arrives one minute after the Edgware train. Thus the Euston train will be the first to arrive only if Sharon happens to arrive at the tube station during this one-minute interval. If she enters the station at any other time, during the nine-minute interval, the Edgware train will come first. Since Sharon's arrival is random, the odds are nine to one in favour of Edgware.

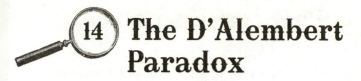

14 The D'Alembert Paradox

No, his reasoning was incorrect. D'Alembert made the error of not carrying through his analysis far enough. The three cases are not equally likely, and the only way to obtain equally likely cases is, in the third case, to toss the coin again even when the first toss is heads, so that the third case has, in fact, two options and becomes the third and fourth cases. The four possible cases are, therefore, as follows:

a) Tails appears on the first toss and again on the second toss.
b) Tails appears on the first toss and heads on the second toss.
c) Heads appears on the first toss and again on the second toss.
d) Heads appears on the first toss and tails on the second toss.

As there are now proved to be four cases and as three of these are favourable, then the probability of heads at least once is, in fact, 3/4.

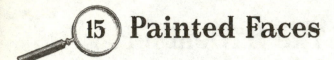

15 Painted Faces

A, B and C are the three philosophers. A thought: "Since B laughs he thinks his face is clean. Since he believes that, if he saw that my face was clean also, he would be astonished at C's laughter, for C would have nothing to laugh at. Since B is not astonished he must think that C is laughing at me. Hence my face is black."

16 Cash Flow

54 pieces.

17 How Long

19.2 yards.

18 The Cloak

The cloak is worth £92. If the cloak is worth x then we know x+100 = 12months and x+20=7months. So x+20 = 7/12ths of x+100, and x=92.

19 Two Steamers

The second, because

$$\frac{x}{30} + \frac{x}{40}$$

is greater than

$$\frac{2x}{35}$$

20 The Orchard

36 apples.

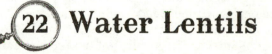

21 Arithmetic Problem

Ten problems.

22 Water Lentils

29 days. For on the second day we actually begin with 2.

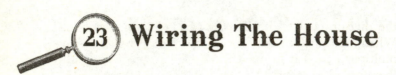

23 Wiring The House

In the basement Timothy fastens any two of the three wires together. He labels the free wire A.

In the attic, Timothy tests every pair of wires with the meter – that is, three possible pairings. The pair the current goes through is the one fastened in the basement. The leftover wire is A's other end and must be labelled A too. Timothy then fastens A to a randomly chosen wire of the pair, which he labels B. The third wire is labelled C.

Back in the basement, Timothy unfastens the two wires and tests all three possible pairs of wires with the meter. The pair with current is fastened in the attic, and the wire not labelled A must be labelled B. The third is labelled C.

24 The Long Division

First, observe that the five-digit quotient forms only three products with the divisor. Therefore two of the five digits must consist of 0s. These cannot be the first or last, since both obviously form products. They are therefore the second and fourth digits, those covered by the white bishops. Furthermore, the two-digit divisor, when multiplied by 8, gives a two-digit product; but when multiplied by another number, the one concealed under the first white rook, it gives a three-digit product; therefore the hidden multiplier must be larger than 8, consequently 9. Both the first and last digits in the quotient give three-digit products with the two-digit divisor, wherefore both must be 9's. We now have established the quotient: it is 90,809. Let us find the divisor, covered up beneath the two white knights. When multiplied by 8 it forms a two-digit product; when multiplied by 9 it forms a three-digit product. It must, therefore, be 12; 8 x 12 = 96, 9 x 12 = 108; neither 10, 11, 13 nor any larger number meets these requirements. The numbers under the remaining chess pieces are readily found.

25 The Truel

The poorest shot, the Baron of Rockall, has the best chance of surviving. Lord Montcrief, the one who never misses, has the second best chance. Because the Baron's two opponents will aim at each other when their turns come, his best strategy is to fire into the air until one of the others is killed. He will then get the first shot at the survivor, which gives him the advantage.

26 Missiles On Target

Since the two missiles approach each other with a combined speed of 30,000 miles per hour, or 500 miles per minute, one minute before the collision the missiles would have to be 500 miles apart.

27 Fair Shares

There are several procedures by which N persons can divide a cake into N pieces so that each person is satisfied that he has got at least 1/N of the cake. The following method has the advantage of leaving no excess pieces of cake.

Assume four people are sharing the cake. Call them A, B, C and D. First A cuts off what he is content to keep as his $\frac{1}{4}$ of the cake. Next B has the option, if he thinks A's slice is more than $\frac{1}{4}$, of reducing it by cutting off some of it. If B thinks A's slice is $\frac{1}{4}$ or less, he does nothing. C, D and E in turn then have an opportunity to do the same with A's slice. The last person to touch this slice keeps it as his share. If anyone thinks that this last person has less than 1/4 he is naturally pleased because it means, in his eyes, that more than 3/4 remains. The remainder of the cake, including any cut-off pieces, is now divided among the remaining three persons in the same manner, then among two. The final division is made by one person doing the cutting and the other the choosing. This procedure can be applied to any number of persons.

28 Generosity

$x=$ $y=$

At first there were twenty people, and each received $60. Then, fifteen persons (five fewer) would have received $80 each. But twenty-four (four more) appeared and only received $50 each.

$$x \cdot y = (x-5)(y+20) = (x+4)(y-10)$$

29 The Striking Clock

4 seconds – the time between the clapper striking the bell for the first peal and the second one is 2 seconds, 2 seconds later it strikes for the third peal. Do not be confused by the lingering sound – I said strike!

30 The River

2 and $^2/_3$ minutes (2 minutes 40 seconds).

Speed downstream 1 km per minute. Speed back $^1/_2$ km per minute. Therefore the current makes a quarter of a km per minute difference, so his boat speed is three-quarters of a km per minute. 2 km divided by three quarters of a km per minute equals two and two-thirds minutes.

31 Racing Driver

Av Speed = $\dfrac{\text{distance}}{\text{time}}$

160 mph. (The secret lies in converting miles per hour to miles per minute and in using fractions instead of decimals to avoid rounding errors.)

$$\frac{6\ mi}{\dfrac{3}{140} + \dfrac{1.5}{168} + \dfrac{1.5}{210}} = 160$$

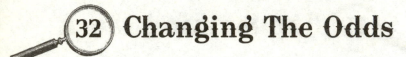

32 Changing The Odds

The boy picked a pebble and, without looking, pretended to drop it inadvertently, where the colour was no longer identifiable. He then pointed out to the king that the colour of the dropped pebble could be ascertained by checking the colour of the one remaining in the hat.

33 Two Cans

Yes. Freeze the water in the two cans before putting it into the empty container.

34 Zeno's Paradox

Achilles would reach the tortoise at one-thousand one hundred and eleven and one-ninth metres. If the race track is shorter than this, the tortoise would win. If it were exactly this size, it would be a tie. Otherwise Achilles will pass the tortoise.

35 Handshakes

Even. The proof is as follows: If you were to ask everyone in the world how many hands he or she has shaken, the total would be even because each handshake would have been counted twice – once each by the two people who shook hands. A group of numbers whose sum is even cannot contain an odd number of odd numbers.

36 The Boy And The Girl

The boy has red hair, the girl black hair. There are four possible combinations: true-true, true-false, false-true, and false-false. It is not the first, since we are told that at least one statement is false. Nor is it the second or third because, in each case, if one lied, then the other could not have been telling the truth. Therefore it is the fourth; both lied.

37 Hats in the Wind

The probability is zero. If nine people have their own hats, then the tenth must too.

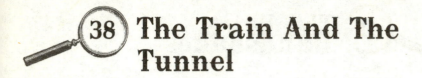

38 The Train And The Tunnel

Two minutes – one minute for the engine and another minute for the last car.

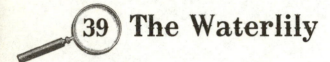

39 The Waterlily

The fifty-ninth day. Since waterlilies double each day, the lake is half covered the day before it is fully covered. (Sometimes it is easier to solve a problem backward than forward.)

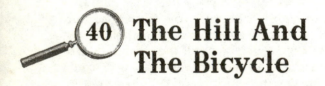

40 The Hill And The Bicycle

The apparent answer – 15 miles an hour – is wrong. The correct answer is 13 $1/3$ miles an hour because speed is determined by dividing distance by time. Notice, incidentally, that the answer is the same no matter how long this hill is.

41 The Brick

Three pounds. If the brick balances with three quarters of a brick and three quarters of a pound, then one quarter of a brick must weigh three quarters of a pound. Thus a whole brick weighs four times as much, or three pounds.

42 A Unique Number

It is the only one that contains all the numerals in alphabetical order.

43 Can You

This statement was made by a salmon fisherman who was asked what he did with all the fish he caught.

44 The Boss And His Chauffeur

For fifty minutes. He saved the chauffeur ten minutes of travelling time each way and thus was picked up at 4:50pm rather than the usual time.

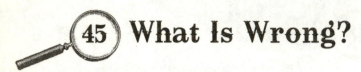

45 What Is Wrong?

Why are these statements obviously untrue?
1) Until the second William, he'd just have been King William
2) Astronauts do not see any sunset in space.
3) The Stars and Stripes was created by the descendent of the Pilgrim Fathers.
4) Before Christ, there was no concept of BC.

46 The Lock

The total number of combinations must be 100,000 as any five-digit number you can think of will be within the range of 00000 and 99999.

47 The Weather Report

The five temperatures were: 1, -1, 2, -2, and 3.

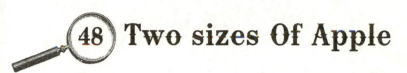

48 Two sizes Of Apple

This is a common trap in mathematical tests. The charge for the apples should be 33⅓ cents for large apples and 20 cents for smaller apples, so the average charge per apple should be

$$\frac{33⅓ + 20}{2} = 26⅔ \text{ cents}$$

and not 25 cents, which the boy collected. If the 60 apples had been sold for 26⅔ cents each, the boy would have received

60 * 26⅔ cents or $16.

The son was charging too little for the apples and the dollar went to the customers.

49 Presidents

If the fifth president were not among those who died on that date, then the newspaper item would almost certainly have made the more impressive statement that, 'Three of the first four presidents died on the Fourth of July.' Therefore, Professor Flugel was reasonably confident that the fifth president, James Monroe, died on that date.

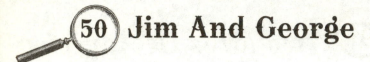

50 Jim And George

They are standing back-to-back.

51 A Chiming Clock

An hour and a half – from 12:15 to 1:45. Once you have heard the clock chime once seven times, you need not wait for it to chime again, for the next cannot be anything but two o'clock.

52 The Half-Full Barrel

All they had to do was tilt the barrel on its bottom rim. Say the barrel was exactly half full. Then when the water is just about to pour out, the water level at the bottom of the barrel should just cover all the rim. That way half the barrel is full of water; the other half is air space.

53 The Scarves

Eleanor would be the best. For rapidity, Eleanor to Marian is 5:2, and Eleanor to Guinevere is 3:4. Lightness gives Guinevere 5:1 over Eleanor and 3:5 to Marian. Warmth tells us that Marian is 4:1 to Guinevere, and 1:3 to Eleanor.

 54 The Marksman

The marksman who fires 5 shots in 5 seconds takes $1\frac{1}{4}$ seconds between shots, since there are 4 intervals between the first and last shots. The other marksman requires 10 seconds for 9 intervals, or $1\frac{1}{9}$ seconds between shots. Therefore, the second marksman will take less time to fire 12 shots - $12\frac{2}{9}$ seconds compared with $13\frac{3}{4}$ seconds.

 55 The Marbles

Only 2 marbles can be transferred out of the first bag. The contents of the 2 bags will then be one of the following:

	First Bag			Second Bag		
	Col A	Col B	Col B	Col A	Col B	Col B
1st possibility	3	3	1	3*	3*	5
2nd possibility	3	2	2	3	4	4

To assure at least 2 of each colour in the first bag, at least 7 marbles must be transferred back, because the first 6 might be the 3 Colour A and the 3 Colour B marbles represented by the starred 3s in the first possibility shown above. Therefore, there will be 4 marbles remaining in the second bag.

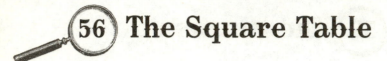

56 The Square Table

Let's examine the problem from the point of view of any one of the woman. Initially, since she is a woman, she reasons that her neighbours' hands would be raised regardless of whether the unseen individual was a man or a woman. But after further thought it occurs to her that if the person opposite was actually a man, he would have known immediately that the person sitting opposite him was a woman because his neighbours would have raised their hands only for that reason. Since the unseen person did not make this announcement, it could only be because she was a woman.

57 A Carbon Copy

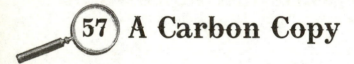

He must start in the lower left corner.

58 Walking In Step

Whenever they step out together, it will always be on the left foot.

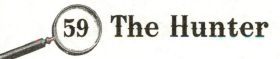

59 The Hunter

If one were to answer without thinking, he would say the first shepherd had 3 piasters and the second 5. After a little thought, one would realise that this is not correct. Why? The 8 piasters was in payment for 8/3 loaves. It follows then, that the equivalent of 8 loaves is 24 piasters, or one loaf is worth 3 piasters. Since each ended up with 22/3 loaves, the first shepherd, who had three loaves to start with, gave 1/3 of a loaf to the hunter; the other 21/3 was given by the other shepherd. Therefore, 1 piaster goes to the first shepherd and 7 to the second.

60 Unusual Equations

(a) 545 + 5 = 550 (Use the hyphen to change the first + into a 4).

(b) $99 + \dfrac{9}{9} = 100$

(c) $\dfrac{7}{0.7} \times \dfrac{7}{0.7} = 100$

This solution is somewhat flawed, as zero is used, and besides, the same principle can be applied to any number, thus:

$$\dfrac{N}{0.N} \times \dfrac{N}{0.N} = 100$$

(d) $\dfrac{9+9}{0.9}$

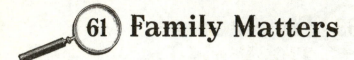

61 Family Matters

The father and mother were both of the same age, thirty-six years old, and the three children were triplets of six years of age. Thus the sum of all their ages is ninety years, and all the other conditions are correctly fulfilled.

62 The Gambler

If he spent one-third, he had two-thirds left. He lost two-thirds of the remainder at dice; two-thirds of two-thirds is four-ninths. Therefore, he spent and lost one-third plus four-ninths = seven ninths. The remainder is two-ninths = 12. If two-ninths of the money is $12, then the original sum must have been $54.

63 Fly Around The World

Suppose that three planes are needed, so that two planes can transfer their fuel at the right moment to the third. Call these A, B, and C. All three start at once from the island with full tanks. When they get one-eighth of the way around the world they have used up one-quarter of their fuel. C then divides its fuel into three equal parts; having three-quarters of its fuel left, it transfers one-quarter to A, one-quarter to B, and uses the remaining one-quarter to fly back to the island. (Notice that all the fuel in its tank is used up.)

A and B now have full tanks again. They fly on till they reach one-quarter of the way around. Both then have three-quarters of their fuel left. B then transfers one-quarter of its fuel to A, because the remaining half is needed so that it can return to base. A full tank, we know, is sufficient to fly halfway. Since A has covered one-quarter of the way with a full tank, it can cover three-quarters of the way. Here it is met by C, who, in the meantime, has refuelled and flown from the island the other way, using the fact that the earth is round. It halves the remainder, so that both reach seven-eighths of the way, where they are met by B. To reach this point, B has used up one-quarter of its fuel. It needs another quarter for the return journey, but divides the remainder between A and C. Now A, B and C can all return to the island, A having successfully flown around the earth.

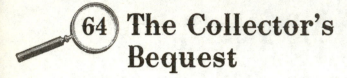

64 The Collector's Bequest

3121:
          3121 - 1 = 3120 x 4/5 =
          2496 - 1 = 2495 x 4/5 =
          1996 - 1 = 1995 x 4/5 =
          1596 - 1 = 1595 x 4/5 =
          1276 - 1 = 1275 x 4/5 =
          1020 ÷ 5 = 204 for each daughter.

65 Jugs

To solve this puzzle you must first investigate the only two possibilities by which you can begin the decanting: you can either pour water into jug B until jug B is full, or pour water into jug C until jug C is full. During the operations you must avoid a situation in which both B and C are entirely full because then the only way to proceed would be to pour the contents of B and C entirely into A – in other words go back to the beginning and start again.

The two possibilities are:

JUG	A	B	C	A	B	C
Commence (pints)	8	0	0	8	0	0
Operation 1	3	5	0	5	0	3
Operation 2	3	2	3	5	3	0
Operation 3	6	2	0	2	3	3
Operation 4	6	0	2	2	5	1
Operation 5	1	5	2	7	0	1
Operation 6	1	4	3	7	1	0
Operation 7	4	4	0	4	1	3
Operation 8				4	4	0

Thus it can be seen that to commence by pouring into jug B until it is full produces the solution with the least number of decantings, which is seven.

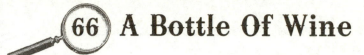

66 A Bottle Of Wine

Hands up everyone who said £1. This is wrong as the total of the bottle of wine will then be £11. The correct answer is 50p.

67 One-Two-Three

Each line of numbers describes the line above it, i.e. 1 then 1-1 then 2-1s then 1-2, 1-1 etc. The next row is 3 1 1 3 1 2 1 1 1 3 1 2 2 1.

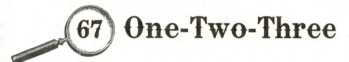

68 Men In A Circle

7 men; 2 shillings.

Let m = number of men, k = number of shillings possessed by the last (i.e. the poorest) man. After one circuit, each is a shilling poorer, and the moving heap contains m shillings. Hence, after k circuits, each is k shillings poorer, the last man now having nothing, and the moving heap contains mk shillings. Hence the thing ends when the last man is again called on to hand on the heap, which then contains (mk + m - 1) shillings, the penultimate man now having nothing, and the first man having (m - 2) shillings. It is evident that the first and last man are the only two neighbours whose possessions can be in the ratio 4 to 1. Hence either

$$mk + m - 1 = 4(m - 2)$$

or else

$$4(mk + m - 1) = m - 2$$

The first equation gives $mk = 3m - 7$, ie $k = 3 - 7/m$, which evidently gives no integral values other than $m = 7, k = 2$.

The second gives $4mk = 2 - 3m$, which evidently gives no positive integral values.

Hence the answer is: 7 men; 2 shillings.

69 Handicap Race

We know from the first race that Man A runs 100 yards in the same time as Man B runs 95 yards. It follows, therefore, that in the second race both men would be neck and neck 5 yards short of the finishing line. As Man A was the faster runner he went on to overtake Man B in the last 5 yards and win the race.

70 Gold Card

It certainly is not! It is 2-1 on that the gambler will win. In other words he will win two games out of three.

We are not dealing with cards here but with sides. There were six sides to begin with, three of each:

GOLD	SILVER
1	
1	
	1
	1
1	1
--	--
3	3

The card on the table cannot be the silver/silver card so eliminate that one and we are left with:

GOLD	SILVER
1	
1	
1	1
--	--
3	1

We can see one gold side so we are left with:

GOLD	SILVER
1	
1	1
--	--
2	1

The reverse side can be GOLD, or GOLD, or SILVER. Odds 2-1 on.

71 The Missing £

We have made a mathematical error here. We are saying that each man spent £9 plus £2 tip between them, but the £27 included the £2 tip.

We should say:

The meal cost	£25
The waiter's tip	£ 2
Change	£ 3
	£30

72 A Digital Puzzle

A decimal point.

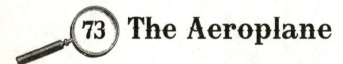

73 The Aeroplane

Since the wind boosts the plane's speed from A to B and retards it from B to A, one is tempted to suppose that these forces balance each other so that total travel time for the combined flights will remain the same. This is not the case, because the time during which the plane's speed is boosted is shorter than the time during which it is retarded, so the overall effect is one of retardation. The total time in a wind of constant speed and direction, regardless of the speed or direction, is always greater than if there were no wind.

74 Drive-By

As Mr. Desborough can walk 27 steps while the car goes 162, the car is clearly going six times as fast as the man. The man walks 3.5 miles an hour: therefore the car was going at 21 miles an hour.

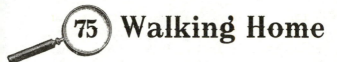

75 Walking Home

Yes. He took as much time for the second half of his trip as the whole trip would have taken on foot. So no matter how fast his first ride was, he lost exactly as much time as he spent on it.

He would have saved time by walking all the way.

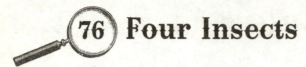

76 Four Insects

10 inches.

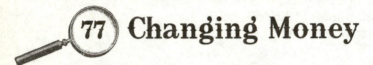

77 Changing Money

It is quite obvious that the economies of Eastland and Westland paid for the razor blades. If Malcolm were to repeat the transaction often enough, the end result would give him all, or a large part, of the stock of razor blades in both countries, together with one Eastland or Westland dollar. The two countries would be left with their stocks of blades largely denuded, but with their domestic currencies repatriated.

For a better understanding of this situation, assume that Malcolm is a money changer, and that one Eastland dollar equals one Westland dollar. If inhabitants of the two countries were to change the currencies back and forth often enough, and Malcolm were to charge 10% commission on each transaction, the end result would give Malcolm all the available cash in Eastland and Westland dollars.

78 A Pair Of Socks

The answer is three. If I pick three socks, then either they are all of the same colour (in which case I certainly have a pair of the same colour) or else two are of one colour and the third is of the other colour, so in that case I would again have a matching pair.

79 The Slow Horses

"Switch horses."

80 Hourglass

Start both hourglasses. When the four-minute glass runs out, turn it over (four minutes elapsed). When the seven-minute glass runs out, turn it over (seven minutes elapsed). When the four-minute glass runs out this time (eight minutes elapsed), the seven-minute glass has been running for one minute. Turn it over once again. When it stops nine minutes have elapsed.

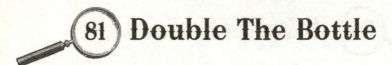

81 Double The Bottle

2 gallons. A volume has three dimensions and each is doubled according to the question. Hence the new volume is 2 x 2 x 2 times the original volume.

82 Sorting the Numbers

The numbers 15, 16 and 17 should be placed in groups 3, 3 and 2, respectively. Group 1 consists of numbers composed entirely of curved lines, Group 2 consists of numbers composed entirely of straight lines, and Group 3 consists of numbers composed of a combination of curved and straight lines.

83 Categories

The categories are as follows:

A M T U V W Y (symmetry about the vertical axis)
B C D E K (symmetry about the horizontal axis)
F G J L N P Q R S Z (no symmetry)

and

H I O X (symmetry about both axes).

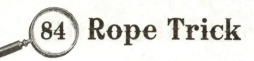

84 Rope Trick

The flagpoles are right next to each other.

85 What Weights

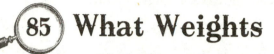

1 pound, 3 pounds, 9 pounds.
   The key to this is that the boy can put any combination of weights on either pan and the difference between the two weights is the amount of fruit he sells. Thus the weight he requires is the result of an addition or subtraction sum.

$$1 - 0 = 1$$
$$3 - 1 = 2$$
$$3 - 0 = 3$$
$$(3 + 1) - 0 = 4$$
$$9 - (3 + 1) = 5$$
$$9 - 3 = 6$$
$$(9 + 1) - 3 = 7$$
$$9 - 1 = 8$$
$$9 - 0 = 9$$
$$(9 + 1) - 0 = 10$$
$$(9 + 3) - 1 = 11$$
$$(9 + 3) - 0 = 12$$

and finally $(9 + 3 + 1) - 0 = 13$

86 How Close

Father.

87 Décaffiné

$33^1/_3$ cups. Because there is 3% caffeine left in the doctored coffee; in 100 cups there would be enough for 3 cups of regular; 3 goes into 100 exactly $33^1/_3$ times.

88 Eggstravaganza

One half, technically. If 1.5 hens lays 1.5 eggs in 1.5 days, then 1 hen lays 1 egg in 1.5 days. A single "better hen by half" will lay 1 egg in 0.75 days. That's 4 eggs in three days, 8 in 6, 12 in 9, and 15 (half a score and half again = 10+5) in 10.5 days (1.5 weeks). One half plus a half is one hen.

89 How Many Hops

... be able to hop out.

You hop $4^1/_2$ feet at the first attempt, which is half-way out, and then another $2^1/_4$ feet at the next hop. Thus you are already three-quarters of the way out in two hops. You feel encouraged, for surely the last quarter will be hopped easily! Let us write down the hops:

$4^1/_2, 2^1/_4, 1^1/_8, ^9/_{32}, ^9/_{64}, ^9/_{128}, ^9/_{256}, ^9/_{512}, ^9/_{1024},$ and so on.

Add these up and you will see that you are nearly there – in fact, you can hop more than $8^3/_4$ feet of the total distance needed of 9 feet. But this is a series whose 'sum to infinity' is less than 9 feet.

90 The Painting

The man's son.

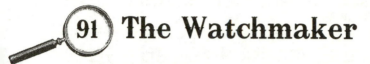

91 The Watchmaker

As the problem says, the apprentice mixed up the clock hands so that the minute hand was short and the hour hand long.

The first time the apprentice returned to the client was about 2 hours and 10 minutes after he had set the clock at six. The long hand moved only from 12 to a little past 2. The short hand made 2 full circles and an additional 10 minutes. Thus the clock showed the correct time.

Next day around 7.05 am he came a second time, 13 hours and 5 minutes after he had set the clock for six. The long hand, acting as hour hand, covered 13 hours to reach 1. The short hand made 13 full circles and 5 minutes, reaching 7. So the clock showed the correct time again.

92 Birthdates

With twenty-four people in the room you would in the long run lose 23 and win 27 out of each 50 bets. (This ignores February 29th.)

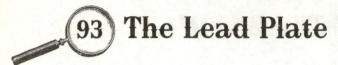

93 The Lead Plate

They poured the shot into the jug and then poured in water, which filled all the spaces between the pellets. Now the water volume plus the shot volume equalled the jar's volume.

Removing the shot from the jar, they measured the volume of water remaining, and subtracted it from the volume of the jar.

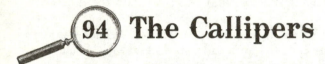

94 The Callipers

He placed an object between one leg and its indentation, so that the callipers could be removed without opening the legs. He then subtracted the length of the object from the spread of the callipers.

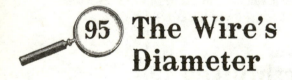

95 The Wire's Diameter

Wind a pre-determined number of coils tightly around a cylinder, on top of each other, so the result is flat, and measure the cylinder with and without the coils. Then subtract the width of the bare cylinder from the width of the coiled cylinder, and divide by the number of coils. So if twenty diameters make 2cm., then 1 diameter is 0.1cm.

96 The Bottle's Volume

The area of a circle, square, or rectangle can easily be calculated after measuring sides or diameter with a ruler. Call the area s.

With the bottle upright, measure the height h1 of the liquid. The full part of the bottle has the volume sh1.

Turn the bottle upside down and measure the height h2 of the air space. The empty part of the bottle has the volume sh2. The whole bottle has the volume s(h1 + h2).

97 The Ship And The Seaplane

Perhaps you can spot without any algebra or extended calculation that the seaplane goes 200 miles, while the ship goes another 20.

98 The Mirror

It does neither – it reverses you back-to-front. If you walk up to a full-length mirror, your face will touch your reflected face, toes touch toes and also your right hand will touch your reflected right hand and the same with left. Now, hold on; your front may be against 'your' front, and back away from back, but according to the compass your right hand is on the east side, your left on the west, head up and feet down, and the same with the reflections, except that you are facing north and the reflection faces south, ie like the spherical mirror, which you can turn top-to-bottom, but not back-to-front. All this shows that the only reason we think we are reflected as changed left-to-right and not top-to-bottom is really based on our usual manner of turning back-to-front. If we were facing south like the reflection and then we turned around to the mirror not keeping upright but flopping over vertically (horizontal axis) with head down at the end, we would find the mirror had reversed our top (our left hand) with our bottom (right hand), and not our left (head) with our right (foot). Thus it's only due to our normal left-to-right way of turning back-to-front, which the mirror has symmetrically done for us. The same would happen if we had a rubber glove, fingers away from us, on a table; if we turn it inside-out without otherwise moving it, thumb would remain on the east side and palm on top, but fingers now toward us.

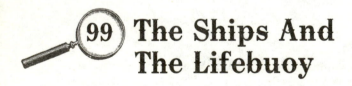

99 The Ships And The Lifebuoy

From the buoy's point of view (floating downstream) the ships move away from it at equal speeds in still water. Then they return at equal speeds in still water. Thus the two ships reach the buoy simultaneously.

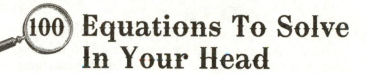

100 Equations To Solve In Your Head

Adding and subtracting the equations, to get two different sets of answers, we see that $10000x + 10000y = 50000$; and $3502x - 3502y = 3,502$. Divide the first by 10,000 and the second by 3,502 to obtain $x+y = 5$ and $x-y = 1$, so $x = 3$ and $y = 2$.

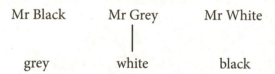

101 Three Men in the Street

The key is that the man in white is talking to Mr Black and so cannot be him. Nor can he be Mr White, since nobody is wearing his own colour. So the man in white must be Mr Grey. We can show what we know like this:

Mr Black	Mr Grey	Mr White
	|	
grey	white	black

Mr Black cannot be wearing black; so he's in white. That leaves Mr White wearing grey.

102 Sisters

They are part of triplets.

103 The Telephone Call

Father and daughter.

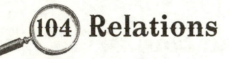

104 Relations

Jill is Jean's mother.

105 Aborigines

The big Aborigine was the mother of the little Aborigine.

106 Sons' Ages

There are only fourteen combinations of ages that correspond with the first and second clues. Since the person solving the puzzle presumably knows his own age, the fact that the second clue isn't sufficient to lead to a solution shows that his age must be thirty-six – the only product that occurs twice. The final clue, revealing that there is only one oldest son and not more, shows that the combination of ages must be 9, 2 and 2.

The Dinner Party

One:

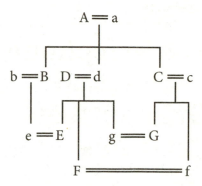

Males = capital letters. Females = small letters.
The Governor is E and the guest is C.

108 Four Families

The maximum possible number of children is 17, as 18 are enough for two baseball teams. Given this condition, several house numbers exist from 24 to 140 which are the product of the children of four families decreasing in size to a minimum of 1. There are also several house numbers from 120 to 240 which are the product of the children of four families decreasing in size to a minimum of 2. The maximum number in the host's cousin's family must be 2; if it were higher than 2, the total for all four families would be 18 or more. When the visitor asked the question, "Does your cousin's family consists of a single child?", he must have known that the house number was 120 because that is the only house number in which the minimum number in the family may be either 1 or 2. However, both the combinations 8, 5, 3, 1 and 6, 5, 4, 1 can equal 120, whereas the only combination including 2 is 5, 4, 3, 2. Therefore, the answer to the question must have been "no" in order for the visitor to be sure that the numbers of children in the families were 5, 4, 3 and 2.

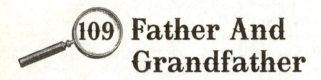

109 Father And Grandfather

Yes. It is perfectly possible for one's maternal grandfather to be younger than one's father.

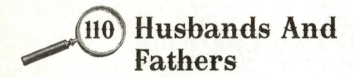

110 Husbands And Fathers

After the deaths of their mothers, Mary married Joan's father and Joan married Mary's father.

111 How Many Children?

There are four boys and three girls.

112 Boys And girls

No, the sultan's law would not work. Of the first children born to all the women, half would be boys and half girls. The mothers of the boys would have no more children. The mothers of the girls would have a second round of children, half of which would be boys and half girls. Again the mothers of the boys would drop out, leaving the other mothers to have a third round of children. Each time, the number of girls would equal the number of boys, so the ratio would never change. Since in any round of births the ratio of boys to girls is one to one, it follows that when you sum the results of all the rounds, the ratio remains one to one throughout.

113 Two Children

Since I have two children, at least one of which is a boy, there are three equally probable cases: Boy-Boy, Boy-Girl or Girl-Boy. In only one case are both children boys, so the probability that both are boys is 1/3.

My sister's situation is different. Knowing that the older child is a girl, there are only two equally probable cases: Girl-Girl or Girl-Boy. Therefore the probability that both children are girls is 1/2.

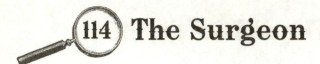

114 The Surgeon

The eight men and John were members of a bomber flight crew during World War II. They had to make an emergency landing on a bare uninhabited island in the South Pacific, far off any sea lanes.

The radio equipment was out of action, and their only hope of being saved was a search operation by the US Air Force or Navy. Weeks passed with ever smaller rations available to sustain life. When all food reserves were exhausted, they had to chose between dying one by one or cannibalising parts of their bodies. They agreed to start with sacrificing their left forearms. John's, being the only surgeon on board, had to be spared to perform the operations. He had to undertake, however, that if they survived he would have his limb amputated within five years after the end of the war.

The five-year span was agreed to give John time to study a different profession.

In the event he changed his mind and decided to use the deception, which he hoped would satisfy his former comrades that he had honoured his vow.

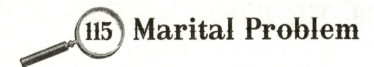

115 Marital Problem

Jason and Dean were both clergyman. Dean married Jason to Denise, which explains why they share the same wedding anniversary. Jason married Jackie to a man whose name happens to be Peter. On another occasion, John married Dean to a girl called Paula.

116 The Widow's Sister

When Eric was 20 he married Joan, who had a sister Betty. Joan died in childbirth three years later whereupon, after a decent interval, Eric wed Betty. When Eric died, Betty became his widow and therefore it could be said of Eric that he had once married his widow's sister.

117 The Lift Stopped

The wife is in the apartment on a life support system, connected to the mains.

118 The Car Crash

The surgeon was Robert Jones' mother.

119 The Barber's Shop

John regularly has assignations with the barber's wife, and wants to ascertain how soon the barber is likely to come home.

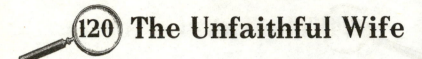

120 The Unfaithful Wife

On Eva's way out, John had noticed a ladder in her left stocking. When she went to the kitchen for coffee he noticed that the ladder was on her right leg.

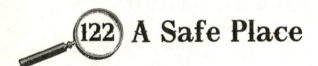

121 The Bridge

Michael set out for B-town as soon as he saw the sentry disappear into his bunker. Timing his progress, he walked for almost 5 minutes. He then turned round and started running back towards A-town. The sentry emerged and, seeing Michael running towards A-town, ordered him to 'return' to B-town.

122 A Safe Place

a) Playing baseball.
b) Catcher.
c) Third base.

123 The Last Movie

They were in a drive-in movie.

124 The Last Letter

She was a skywriter. Lightning struck her plane and she crashed.

125 Death In The Car

The man was in a convertible. He was shot when the top was down.

126 The Stranger

The woman died during childbirth. The stranger in the car is the baby.

127 The Heir

The test was a blood test. The elder remembered that the true prince was a haemophiliac.

128 The Antique Candelabra

The distinguished-looking man appeared to be an expert on 17th century works of art and immediately recognized the candelabra as the work of Girolamo Fabrici.

He knew that the candelabra in the window was one of a pair, and he wanted to buy the pair. He was most disappointed to hear that only one was available and he mentioned that he was prepared to pay £25,000 for the set, but the one piece was of no interest.

Eventually he was persuaded by the antique dealer to buy the one piece for £5,000, while repeating his offer of £20,000 for the second piece, to complete the set.

The dealer, most anxious not to lose the deal, phones round the trade, without success until, two days later, he hears from a colleague that indeed the second candelabra had been offered.

When Robert shows the piece to the dealer, he recognises this to be the genuine article and is glad to pay £9,000 for it.

Needless to add, the distinguished-looking gentleman could no longer be located.

129 A Soldiers Dream

The soldier dreamed when he was supposed to be on guard duty.

130 The Jilted Bride

She had jammed the clapper with packed snow which melted during the ceremony. No one noticed the damp patch below the bell.

131 The Careful Driver

I was travelling in the wrong direction; the cars I passed were all going the other way.

132 The Two Solicitors

Smith's full name was Tracy Smith. Jones had started an affair with Tracy, claiming that he was a bachelor, and had promised to marry her.

133 A Glass of Water

The man had hiccups. The bartender's action, producing a sudden shock, was a quicker-acting cure than a glass of water might have been.

134 The Deadly Scotch

The poison was inside the ice cubes, which dissolved in Lay's drink, but not in El's.

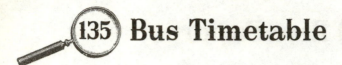

135 Bus Timetable

Every four minutes.

The buses are evenly spaced along the road in both directions. He counts every hour twenty moving in one direction and ten in the opposite direction. There are thirty buses in that section over which he travels in an hour, and half of these buses turn around in the hour. Therefore fifteen must leave the terminus every hour or one bus every four minutes.

136 Above Or Below

The Z goes above the line. The pattern is so simple that many intelligent people miss it: Letters comprised of straight lines go above, letters with curves go below.

137 The Steelworker

David Miller works the night shift at the steelworks and, as he lives in the basement of the high-rise, has to descend the stairs to reach his apartment.

138 Rice Paper

The stack will clearly consist of 2^{50} sheets of paper, which is well over 17 million miles high.

139 The Phone-In

The moderator had just announced, "We are now contacting Mr. and Mrs. Bradley of Alperton for their views." Tom heard the ringing tone and, much to his surprise, a man answered the phone. Tom recognized the voice as that of his friend Michael, whom he had suspected of having an affair with his wife.

(140) My puzzle notes